J

A COWBOY'S LIFE

Vic Kovacs

PowerKiDS
press

Published in 2016 by **The Rosen Publishing Group, Inc.**
29 East 21st Street, New York, NY 10010

Developed and produced for Rosen by BlueAppleWorks Inc.

Art Director: T.J. Choleva
Managing Editor for BlueAppleWorks: Melissa McClellan
Designer: Joshua Avramson
Photo Research: Jane Reid
Editor: Jennifer Way

Illustration & Photo Credits: Cover, p. 8-9, 21, 24 Charles Marion Russell/
Public Domain; title page Gift of the Birmingham Public Library;
cover, title page, back cover (skull) Jim Parkin/Shutterstock; cover,
title page (wood) Dagmara_K/Shutterstock; back cover background
homydesign/Shutterstock; background siro46 /Shutterstock; chapter
intro backgrounds rangizzz/Shutterstock; p. 4, 26 Frederic Remington/
Public Domain; p. 6 Time Life Books/Public Domain; p. 10 U.S. National
Archives and Records Administration/Public Domain; p. 14, 16, 17 Carlyn
Iverson; p. 16-17 bottom William Henry Jackson/Gift-State Historical
Society of Colorado; p. 18 Detroit Photographic Co./Public Domain;
p. 28 Regien Paassen/Shutterstock

Cataloging-in-Publication-Data
Kovacs, Vic.
A cowboy's life / by Vic Kovacs.
p. cm. — (The true history of the Wild West)
Includes index.
ISBN 978-1-4994-1169-0 (pbk.)
ISBN 978-1-4994-1199-7 (6 pack)
ISBN 978-1-4994-1190-4 (library binding)
1. Cowboys — West (U.S.) — History — 19th century — Juvenile
literature. 2. West (U.S.) — History — 1860-1890 — Juvenile literature.
3. West (U.S.) — Social life and customs — 19th century — Juvenile
literature. I. Title.
F596.K68 2016
978'.02—d23

Manufactured in the United States of America

CPSIA Compliance Information: Batch #WS15PK
For Further Information contact: Rosen Publishing, New York, New York at 1-800-237-9932

CONTENTS

Chapter 1
What Is a Cowboy?....................5

Chapter 2
Spanish Origins....................7

Chapter 3
The Rise of the Cattle Industry 11

Chapter 4
Cattle Drives 19

Chapter 5
Bygone Era 27

Glossary 30

For More Information 31

Index 32

Although the pay was low, the cowboy was seen as a romantic, heroic figure.

What Is a Cowboy?

A cowboy works on a **ranch**, herding cattle, caring for horses, and fixing fences and buildings. Cowboys work on horseback much of the time.

Cowboys have been riding the range in the American West for more than 150 years. About 10,000 are working today on ranches and in rodeos.

Cowboys often started learning their skills as young as age 12 or 13. Though the first cowboys were Mexican, people of many cultures, including African Americans and Native Americans, were attracted to this rugged way of life in the nineteenth century. These men faced less discrimination on the open range, because a cowboy was valued for his skills more than anything else. Other cowboys were soldiers who had served in the Civil War and headed west looking for work.

Although most cowboys were men, some cowgirls worked on ranches and in rodeos. There are still cowgirls working today, too.

The first cowboys were Mexican vaqueros.
Vaqueros taught their skills to settlers in
Texas and New Mexico.

Spanish Origins

Cowboys first rode up to what is now U.S. territory from Mexico to help settlers with ranches in Texas and New Mexico. In Mexico, cowboys were called **vaqueros**, which describes men who work with cattle. The word comes from *vaca*, which means "cow" in Spanish. The Mexican vaqueros taught the settlers about cattle, horses, and ranching, and the settlers adopted many of their ways. By 1725, the word "cowboy" was being used in English. The traditional image of the cowboy, in his broad-brimmed hat, was well established by 1849.

The vaquero tradition first came to Mexico with the Spanish settlers who had started arriving in the sixteenth century. In many areas of Spain, cattle were raised on large ranches called haciendas. As in Mexico, these areas had a dry climate, so there was not a lot of grass.

The cattle had to graze on large parcels of land in order to get enough to eat. Vaqueros would ride on horseback along with the herds of cattle to make sure they were safe and going the right way. The vaquero way of life was easily adapted to Mexico and to other Spanish colonies in North America.

When English-speaking settlers started arriving in Texas and the Southwest in the nineteenth century, the two cultures combined and the American cowboy

The most important part of a cowboy's work on cattle runs was making sure that cows did not break away from the herd.

emerged. In fact, many typical cowboy words come from Spanish, such as "lasso" and "lariat."

Cowboys played an important role in the westward expansion of the United States. They made it possible for ranchers to get millions of cows to market in cities whose growth depended on the cattle trade, such as Kansas City, Kansas, and St. Louis, Missouri. As settlers continued to move west and north, cowboys adapted to the colder weather and worked in the Rocky Mountains and the Dakota territory, too.

9

Cowboys played a key role in the cattle trade, which was important to the growth of many cities in the United States.

The Rise of the Cattle Industry

The cattle industry in America has a long history, dating all the way back to the late 1400s. The first Europeans to come to America brought along herds of longhorn cattle. These early herds were added to over the next two hundred years, first by Spanish settlers, then by Portuguese traders, and finally in large numbers by English immigrants. Cattle herds first began to move west with Spanish missionaries, who settled in western North America and built their missions. The westward spread of cattle really took off after the American Revolution, when more Americans began moving further and further west in North America. Until the mid-nineteenth century, North American cattle were bred mostly for their milk and their hides. They were not generally raised for beef because wild game was plentiful.

MYTH: Cowboys rode alone.

TRUTH OR MYTH? This is a myth. On the trail cowboys worked together as a crew. One reason is that the sheer number of cattle they were driving would have been impossible for just one cowboy to control. Another is that the trail was full of dangers, such as cattle rustlers, and a single cowboy would have been very easily outnumbered in a fight.

By the time Texas became independent from Mexico in 1836, cattle ranches were common all across the west. In Texas, the departing Mexicans often left their herds, which American farmers were quick to claim. By the end of the Civil War in 1865, beef was beginning to become more popular, and as a result cattle prices were on the rise, especially in the Northern states. This helped Southern states to rebuild their shattered postwar economy, but there was still one problem: how to get the cattle from the southernmost parts of the country to the northernmost. This is how cattle drives in the Wild West began.

Joseph McCoy and the Chisolm Trail

Joseph McCoy was a Chicago businessman. He knew that the railroads wanted to improve their business by shipping more freight, and he knew that folks back east had a growing hunger for beef. So, he thought, why not use trains to ship cattle from down south, process it in his Chicago **stockyard**, and then ship the finished product east?

There was just one problem. Farmers in Kansas and Missouri, where most of the railheads were, didn't like Texas cowboys driving herds through their land. This was because Texas longhorn cattle had ticks that spread a deadly disease to other livestock. In 1867, McCoy persuaded the Kansas Pacific Railway to put in a stop just outside the **quarantine** area. There he built a stockyard and loading areas, along with a bank and a hotel. This little village was named Abilene, Kansas, and it was one of the first of many "cow towns" in the Wild West.

Abilene was fed by a route called the Chisholm Trail. The trail was in use between 1867 and 1884; in that time it was used to transport around five million head of cattle.

Jesse Chisholm

Jesse Chisholm is the man for whom the Chisholm Trail is named. He had a gift for languages, and eventually learned over a dozen different Native American dialects. This served him well in his career as a trader, and he also became well known as an interpreter. The trail that bore his name was created when he drove a wagon from Fort Leavenworth, Kansas, to establish a new trading post just outside of Oklahoma City. This journey left clear wagon tracks, which Texas cowboys noticed and followed into Kansas. Even though the Chisholm Trail is most famous as a cattle trail, Chisholm himself never drove livestock along it. He used it only for transporting goods.

Feeder trails all over Texas would lead to the Red River crossing into Oklahoma, where the Chisholm Trail began. It then led north through Native American territory, up to Kansas. The cattle would then be dropped in Abilene, or later, Wichita or Dodge City, where they would begin their journey east.

Goodnight-Loving Trail

While the Chisholm Trail helped to supply the East with cattle, the Goodnight-Loving Trail was blazed to take cattle to the West. Established by former Texas Ranger Charles Goodnight and experienced cowboy Oliver Loving, the trail ran about 2,000 miles (3,219 km). Starting in Young County, Texas, the trail ran southwest to Horsehead Crossing, where it turned north to follow the Pecos River through New Mexico to Denver, Colorado. The trail was later extended to Cheyenne in Wyoming.

On their first drive in 1866, Goodnight and Loving brought about 2,000 head of cattle, along with 18 armed cowboys for protection. They were able to sell most of the cattle to the United States government at Fort Sumner in New Mexico. Goodnight then returned to Texas to get more cattle, while Loving went north to the railhead in Denver.

In 1867, Loving was caught in a Comanche ambush and died two weeks later as a result of his injuries. Goodnight later honored his partner's last wish to be buried in Texas by bringing his body home in a coffin made out of flattened tin cans.

Charles Goodnight

Born in Illinois on March 5th, 1836, Charles Goodnight moved to Texas with his family at the age of ten. By the age of 20, he was a Texas Ranger. During his time with the rangers, he acted mostly as a scout, first in the Texas–Indian Wars, and later in the Civil War. Goodnight is credited with inventing the **chuck wagon**, a kind of mobile kitchen that became a staple of cattle drives. He also preserved a herd of bison on a ranch he founded. He did this during a time when bison were being overhunted, and his wife, fearing their extinction, urged him to set aside part of his ranch to keep a herd.

Cowboys drove cattle along trails that led to railroad stations.

John Ware

Legendary cowboy John Ware was born into slavery around 1845 in South Carolina. After gaining his freedom at the end of the Civil War, he traveled to Texas, where he discovered his destiny on the back of a horse. In 1882, he joined a cattle drive to what would later become Alberta, Canada. With cowboys in demand in that area, and with his incredible skills, Ware easily found work on local ranches. Ware started his own ranch in 1890, and was an integral figure in establishing Alberta's now thriving ranching industry. This would have been an accomplishment for anyone, but for a black man to become a respected and revered member in a nearly all-white community during a time of great racial inequality is truly the stuff of legend.

The heyday of the American cowboy was during the height of cattle drives in the West.

Cattle Drives

The purpose of a cattle drive was to herd large numbers of cattle from ranches to the closest railhead. The railhead was the southernmost point of a railway. Railheads were found in towns such as Dodge City and Wichita, Kansas. Trains would then take the cattle the rest of the way north, often to stockyards in Chicago.

Trail lengths varied, with longer routes like the Goodnight-Loving Trail covering more than 2,000 miles (3,219 km). Drives could last anywhere from 20 days to several months. For maximum profitability a drive would take as many head of cattle as they could, often well over 2,000. A typical crew had from 10 to 15 members. The highest-ranking person on a drive was the trail boss. Sometimes he was the owner of the herd, sometimes not, but he had always ridden the trail before. Thanks to his knowledge and experience on the trail, he knew the best routes to take.

MYTH: Cowboys wore bandannas and wide-brimmed "cowboy" hats.

TRUTH OR MYTH? This is true. Life on the range was sunny and dusty. The cowboy wore his hat to keep off the hot Sun. The bandanna could be pulled over the mouth to keep out some of the dust kicked up by the cattle as they moved along.

After the trail boss, the most important individual was the cook. The cook not only prepared all the meals, but he was also often the closest thing to a doctor the crew had. The majority of the cowboys were the **drovers**, who kept their assigned section of the cattle herd in order. There were different positions for drovers, which indicated their experience and skill. The best drovers rode closest to the front. Finally, there was the wrangler, who managed the remuda, which were the crew's spare horses. The wrangler was usually the least experienced cowboy on the drive, but his was still a big job, since everyone on the crew had eight to ten spare horses.

A Typical Day on the Trail

Days on the trail started early. Rising before dawn, the cook, (or "Cookie," as they were sometimes called), was the first one up to prepare everyone's breakfast. Once it was ready he would bellow out a wake-up call, and all the cowboys got up to eat. Once they were done eating, the cowboys would choose their first mount of the day. Two cowboys would relieve the men who had been the last ones on guard duty the previous night so that they could eat and get fresh horses.

> Although the cook was not driving cattle, he faced many of the same dangers and misfortunes as the cowboys on the trail.

Once everyone had eaten and packed their bedrolls in the chuck wagon, the cook would get a head start on everyone else so that he was set up at the lunchtime meeting spot before everyone else arrived. The trail boss followed the cook, scouting for water and grass along the way. He also kept an eye out for dangers and obstacles. Then the rest of the crew would take their positions and start a day on the trail.

The most trusted cowboys took position at the front of the herd. This position was known as point. They directed the herd along the path the trail boss had picked out. After the point came the swing, near the middle of the herd, and the flank, near the back. Both of these positions were responsible for keeping the herd together and moving. They also went after any strays that left their part of the line. Bringing up the rear was the drag, the worst position in the line. Drag riders had to make sure the weakest members of the herd kept pace, while breathing all the dust kicked up by the entire herd. This job often fell to the least experienced cowboys. Each of these positions had two cowboys each, one on either side of the herd. The exception to this was drag, which had three cowboys.

MYTH: The life of the cowboy was easy and free.

TRUTH OR MYTH? This is a myth. The life of a cowboy was very tough. Cowboys rode the trail all day, often in tough conditions like blazing sun, pouring rain, or even in hailstorms. They were never able to get a full night's sleep, as they would have to get up at some point for night guard duty. On top of that there was the danger of being attacked by rustlers.

The crew usually stopped twice a day. The first stop was around noon, for lunch. As well as eating, cowboys would switch horses, and the cattle could rest, water, and graze. The second stop was around 5:00 p.m., and was at the spot the trail boss had chosen to camp out at for the night.

Next, the cook got dinner going, and the rest of the crew often sang songs or told stories. When the Sun started to set, the first night guards would put the cattle to bed by circling the cattle to smaller and smaller spirals. The rest of the cowboys would bed down, desperate to grab some shuteye before it was their turn as guard.

The Roundup

The gathering of cattle in the Wild West was known as the roundup. There were usually two roundups a year: first in the spring and again in the fall. The goal of a roundup was to bring together all of the cattle of one particular ranch. Cowboys would ride all over their ranch, looking for strays and **stragglers**. In Texas, most ranches were fairly large and spaced far apart, so the roundup was a pretty simple affair. In ranch communities farther north, like those found in Montana, herds would often mingle. As a result, ranchers would have to herd all of the cattle to a particular area, and then sort their individual herds by brand.

> **Roundups are a time for ranches to count, sort, and inspect their cattle.**

Cattle Branding

Cattle branding was the main method ranchers and cowboys used to identify cattle belonging to their herd. A brand was placed on a cow by heating a branding iron in a fire until it was red hot, and then pressing it onto the flesh of the cow. Every ranch had its own unique brand, which could consist of letters, numbers, shapes, or symbols. One of the first skills a cowboy learned was how to read these brands. In the United States, branding was passed on to cowboys by their predecessors, the Mexican vaqueros.

In Texas, the spring roundup was the first step of any cattle drive. During spring roundup, any new calves that had been born since the last roundup would be branded, and the mature stock would be brought together to begin their journey north. Northern ranches didn't usually ship their cattle until the fall roundup, so the spring was used to brand new calves, round up strays, and count how many cattle they currently had. In the fall the northern and southern ranches switched goals, with Texas using the fall to round up strays, and the northern ranches rounding up their stock for shipment and sale.

The development of barbed wire fencing
brought an end to the era of the open range
and large cattle drives.

Bygone Era

The heyday of the cowboy did not last long. It spanned just about twenty years, from 1866 to 1886. The march of progress brought it to an end. During those twenty years, the railroads expanded rapidly, and by the 1890s they reached all the way south to Texas. It was no longer necessary for cowboys to go on long, dangerous journeys to deliver cattle, so the great cattle drives ended, and the famous trails fell into disuse.

Another innovation that completely changed how things were done was the rise of **barbed wire** fences. These fences put a stop to the open range, because ranchers could now clearly define their property and keep their herds together far more easily. Large numbers of cowboys were no longer needed to patrol the range and keep ranchers' herds together, so many cowboys lost their jobs. The ones who remained had to learn how to mend fences as an integral part of their job.

Today cowboy skills can be seen on display at rodeos.

Today, cowboys are still around, just in much smaller numbers than they used to be. They mostly work on ranches, doing many of the same jobs they did more than a hundred years ago. Their list of duties often depends on the size of the ranch. On smaller ranches with fewer cowboys, they're generally jacks-of-all-trades, mending fences, patrolling the range, feeding livestock, and herding cattle. However, it might be more common to see a cowboy patrolling the range in an **all-terrain vehicle**, and he might keep his rifle in a pickup truck instead of in a holster on a horse.

Rodeo

Outside of the ranch, one of the main places the cowboy way still lives on is the rodeo. Rodeo is a competitive sport based on skills that cowboys would have used on the open range. Early rodeos were competitions between cowboys and vaqueros and were simply informal contests to test their skills against each other.

Today, rodeo is a professional sport. Events consist of two types: timed events and "rough stock" events. Popular timed events include roping events, such as calf roping. The object of calf roping is to lasso a calf with a lariat from horseback, and then dismount and tie the calf's legs together in the shortest time possible. Another popular and extremely dangerous timed event is steer wrestling. In this event, a cowboy jumps from the back of his horse to the back of a steer and wrestles it to the ground by grabbing its horns. Rough stock events include **bronco** and bull riding, in which a cowboy tries to stay on a bucking bronco or bull for eight seconds.

Today's brave rodeo performers are keeping the cowboy spirit of the Wild West alive and in people's minds.

Glossary

all-terrain vehicle An open vehicle with large tires designed for rugged terrain.

barbed wire A type of wire with small sharp points of wire spaced in short intervals along the main wire.

bronco An untrained horse that will buck to get a rider off of its back. Broncos are used in rodeos.

chuck wagon A wagon driven by the cook on a cattle trail. It held the crew's supplies. The back of it was called the chuck box, and this held the cook's ingredients for meals, as well as any medical supplies he might need.

drover A person who moves groups of cattle or sheep from one place to another.

lariat Also known as a lasso, it is a strong loop of rope that can be thrown around an object and tightened by pulling on it. It is often used to subdue livestock.

quarantine The act of isolating those known to be diseased in an effort to stop the spread of infection.

ranch a large area of land that is kept for the purpose of raising livestock.

stockyard A space used for gathering and holding livestock for the short term, before the animals are shipped or slaughtered.

stragglers People or animals that have wandered away from the main group.

vaquero Spanish for cowboy.

For More Information

Further Reading

Adkins, Jan. *What If You Met a Cowboy?*
New York, NY: Roaring Brook Press, 2013.

Hicks, Peter. *You Wouldn't Want
to Live in a Wild West Town!*
New York, NY: Scholastic, 2013.

Lassieur, Allison. *The Wild West: An
Interactive History Adventure.*
Mankato, MN: Capstone Press, 2009.

Murray, Stuart. *Wild West.*
New York, NY: DK Eyewitness Books, 2005.

Websites

Due to the changing nature of Internet links,
PowerKids Press has developed an online list of websites
related to the subject of this book. This site is updated
regularly. Please use this link to access the list:
www.powerkidslinks.com/thoww/cowboys

Index

A
African Americans 5

B
barbed wire fences 27

C
cattle drive 17, 19, 25
cattle industry 11
Chisholm, Jesse 14
Chisholm Trail 13, 14, 15
Civil War 5, 12, 16, 17

D
Dakota territory 9
drovers 20

G
Goodnight, Charles 15, 16
Goodnight-Loving Trail 15, 19

H
horses 5, 7, 20, 21, 23

K
Kansas 9, 13, 14, 19

L
lariat 9, 29
lasso 9, 29

M
McCoy, Joseph 13
Mexican 5, 6, 7, 25
Mexico 6, 7, 8, 12, 15
Missouri 13

N
Native Americans 5
New Mexico 6, 7, 15

R
railroads 13, 27
ranch 5, 16, 17, 24, 25, 28, 29
Rocky Mountains 9
rodeo 29
roundup 24, 25

S
soldiers 5
Spain 7

V
vaqueros 6, 7, 8, 25, 29

W
Ware, John 17